Future Shock to Poly Crisis

Moving from Coping to Thriving in an Accelerating World

This book is a guide to navigate the complexities of a rapidly changing world and interrelated crises. It offers insights, strategies, and inspiration for readers looking to thrive in the face of uncertainty and challenges.

From Future Shock to PolyCrisis

Introduction to Futures Thinking

Charlotte Kemp

Published by Charlotte Kemp, 2024.

FROM FUTURE SHOCK TO POLYCRISIS

First edition. August 29, 2024.

Copyright © 2024 Charlotte Kemp.

ISBN: 979-8230007432

Written by Charlotte Kemp.

Preface

One of my highest personal values is that of agency. It's not a common expression but it refers to the capacity of people to make independent choices and to take personal action. It means freedom, within a society's rules. It implies autonomy and the power to chart one's own future.

To get to the future we want we need to navigate through a few stages.

1. Understanding where we are and what uncertainty or stresses we anticipate
2. How we manage to cope with the demands of life
3. How we could get beyond coping by developing adaptive strategies
4. How we could go even further than that by intentionally learning to thrive

We have this privilege, the advantage to explore this progression and see our lives move in a new direction. Many people do not have that advantage. The agency over their own lives, their choices, have been taken out of their hands. And if we don't intentionally act on our own futures, we risk leaving the outcomes to someone else's agenda.

Chapter 1: Introduction

A Cloud of Dread

A family member phoned me in the middle of the day in the middle of a work week. He said that ever since that morning a slight discomfort had been growing in him. He felt unsettled, concerned, aware that something was wrong but unaware of what it could be. We went through several options. "Was it something at home, perhaps a disagreement with family?" No. "Was there tension in the office?" No. "A little unprocessed road rage perhaps?" We explored that, but No. So he turned the questions on himself. "Have I forgotten something that is important? Am I upset with someone? Do I feel guilty about something?"

We explored all of these real and potential situations that could cause his disquiet but none of them seemed to be the cause. He was just trapped in a vague, amorphous cloud of undefined dread. It made every interaction that day, every part of his work just a little more difficult, just a little less pleasant than what he normally experienced.

This was a significant time ago, before the time when social media news feeds could serve up reams of bad news, inflammatory headlines and dramatic attempts for attention. This was before the time that we couldn't leave the house without our cellphones. This was before the present time when it is so easy to be aware of every bit of bad news everywhere around the world.

These days it is very easy to get enveloped in that cloud of disquiet. Perhaps like me you sometimes experience a sudden feeling of alarm. Nothing in your current physical location has changed so you mentally scroll back through your day and try to work out which of the many electronic alerts has seeped into your unconscious and made itself at home. It could be something on social media that you scrolled past in a fraction of a second but which has still managed to penetrate your brain. Maybe it was an alert on your phone or a glance at an unwelcome message. Or perhaps it is the few words you saw in the preview window on your email program.

As I have become more mindful and aware of the physical toll of constant stress and cortisol, I have tried to reset my emotions regularly throughout the day. And only with that intentional attention to my emotions have I realised how often we are incited to anxiety each day. We can see people become vaguely unhinged because of the constant demand for attention, the expectation that we need to be on duty 24/7, the unfiltered data that is fed into our brains every moment of the day.

That disquiet that my family member experienced so long ago, with no real cause other than the pressures of life, is what I see around me, in family and colleagues, of all ages, and all around the world.

While we are attempting to navigate this inner turmoil we are not in a position to enjoy our lives, to create meaningful work, to develop significant relationships. We are just trying to cope, only just holding on. That is the saddest realisation, that the goal of so many people is simply to get through the day, week or month. They have no hope of anything more than that and worse still, that many people never become aware of this state that they are in.

That is why this idea of Future Shock and Poly Crisis is so personal for me. I have fought to redefine my life to get past the shock and crisis and to relish every day. And I went through the stages we will explore here: from realisation, to coping with the situation, to proactively adapting to make progress and then to finding that wonderful place where I feel I can thrive.

I invite you to explore this together with me.

# Introducing Toffler and Tooze

From Alvin Toffler's 1970 book on the stress of rapid change to Adam Tooze's 2022 analysis of a global situation where combined crises pose a great threat, we recognise the legitimate anxiety many feel about the world. In this book we provide strategies to alleviate stress, regain control over the future, and move forward with confidence.

It's not uncommon to hear people complain that nothing makes sense any longer. Values, expectations, behaviour, technologies, the basic building block of society are unfamiliar, confusing and bewildering.

Our response to this senselessness is going to lie somewhere on a continuum from Denial to Sense making.

Denial leaves us victim to ever increasing confusion. Sense making gives us back our agency, our chance to respond, to anticipate and to build resilience.

"I've come up with a set of rules that describe our reactions to technologies:

> *1. Anything that is in the world when you're born is normal and ordinary and is just a natural part of the way the world works.*

2. Anything that's invented between when you're fifteen and thirty-five is new and exciting and revolutionary and you can probably get a career in it.

3. Anything invented after you're thirty-five is against the natural order of things."

Douglas Adams, The Salmon of Doubt

Chapter 2: Future Shock. Shattering Stress.

— 66 ——————————————————

"Future Shock is the shattering stress and disorientation we induce in individuals by subjecting them to too much change in too short a time."
Alvin Toffler

Where it started

I have two very tenuous connections with Alvin Toffler's work. I started reading his books long before I knew there was a field called 'Futures Thinking'. When I started studying this field some time back, my first step was to join the Association of Professional Futurists (APF). When a field is still relatively young one finds that the big names that we read and study are actually still around and members of the same organisation! A few months after I joined APF Alvin Toffler passed away and our association's news feed became filled with stories and anecdotes from people who knew and had worked with him. As a relative newcomer at the time seeing these warm stories and shared insights made me value this community of futurists and my place among them.

And the other reason why I am drawn to this work is the absurd tendency of humans to assign meanings to things in their lives that we insist be interpreted as a synchronicity. Future Shock was published in the same year as my birth, 1970. (I will wait while you do the maths.) When I consider how relevant Toffler's ideas still are for today I always relate it to how I, at my current age, am experiencing the future and how well I may be responding to the rapid changes.

Death of Permanence. Rise of Transience

Alvin Toffler, with his wife Heidi Toffler, explored the nature of rapid change in the world as we move toward the future. Accelerated innovation, the death of permanence and the new transient lifestyle, the pace of life, and changes in society's values all lead to this shattering stress and disorientation.

Technological developments have opened the doors of imagination for people to make novel choices that were not available to previous generations. As these drivers of change evolve and interact with each other, people can have more freedom to choose where to live, how to work, what career they can move into next, how to be in relationship with each other and their local society, and how they define their own identity.

This is equally as valid today as it was when Toffler wrote about it over 50 years ago in 1970. It is equally as valid, but perhaps way more intense. What would he say about the ever more rapid changes in our world today after complaining about the rate of change in the 60s and 70s.

The psychological effect he was exploring was how humans respond to these changes. Are we able to cope with moving to a new city for work, and leaving behind a town where generations of our families have lived? Are we able to reskill ourselves, to keep learning so that we remain relevant for employment? Does the ease of getting into and out of relationships mean that they are healthier or that we are less healthy for them? Does the impermanence of a throw-away society mean that we value things, places or people less?

Toffler also explored the potential benefits of some of these issues. Innovation and creativity can find expression when freed from the shackles of tradition. Entrepreneurship evolves from the dynamic nature of business. Liberated from strict and imposed identities, people can explore more diversity. This diversity of people and of perspective implies more interesting and valuable contributions to society.

Stress and Disorientation

While some people thrive in a fast paced, ever changing world, the process to introduce change implies an introduction of chaos, disruption and disorientation.

Even where we want to experience change, the process of achieving it is difficult and when that change is imposed on us by society, governments, legislation, or technological advances we don't always respond in helpful ways.

This is at the heart of this entire conversation. When the rate of change around us exceeds our capacity to adapt and respond, we experience stress and disorientation. In a state of stress people are not at their best. Their emotions are uncontrolled, their decision making impaired, they have physical symptoms of stress. This is not the best state to be in to take advantage of opportunities, or even to recognise them.

The impact of vast advances

Having more choice and more information has become a major hindrance rather than an aid. The cognitive stress of trying to consider all the ramifications and all of the sources of data is overwhelming. It leads to bad decision making and feeds into confirmation bias.

Algorithms

Social media can provide a good example of how an increase in the availability of information does not necessarily lead to better decisions. In our offline as well as online lives, we act according to algorithms. We operate by using decision making heuristics or rules. We recognise and respond to patterns. We make decisions using intuition which has been fed by our own experiences and prejudices. We make friends with people around us. We filter out information that doesn't relate to us.

The more we do that in our offline lives, the more evident it is in our online world. The newsfeed algorithms will consistently provide us the information we want and expect. As soon as the platform has learned our preferences it will serve up what we want to consume. It doesn't challenge us with contrary points of view or opinions. It doesn't show us voices from the other side of the aisle.

To manage the vast amount of information available to be consumed our technologies provide us only with what we already want to know, what we already believe in. This makes us believe that the world is in harmony with our values.

And that leads us to extreme polarisation of everything. Politics, religion, values, identity, economics, climate, celebrities, the British Royal Family. We will see what we believe to be true. And that leads to reality-TV style family dinners when you realise your cousins are living in a completely different streaming service from yourself.

While Toffler didn't predict social media and its impact, he knew that more information does not necessarily imply better decision making. We aren't making more informed decisions. We are making more reinforced decisions.

Chapter 3: Poly Crisis. Interconnected Challenges

A new way to describe global issues

Sometimes one comes across a word or phrase that is saturated with meaning. 'Future Shock' doesn't need a whole book to explain what it is. We immediately resonate with the concept. And the phrase 'Poly Crisis' is another expression that is intuitively understood. The first time I came across this phrase I immediately imagined a connection with Future Shock. They are not book end concepts, it's not like they demonstrate a beginning and an ending, but more that they are very prominent sign posts on a journey that becomes faster, more complex and less manageable. If we started with Future Shock, we are experiencing Poly Crisis? What comes next? Will we be able to keep up?

The phrase 'polycrisis' was word of the year for 2022 in Collins dictionary and the year 2023 has been called the 'year of polycrisis'. Re-introduced by historian professor Adam Tooze in recent years, polycrisis demonstrates how multiple interconnected crises can create a complex, interdependent system.

"A polycrisis is not just a situation where you face multiple crises. It is a situation ..., where the whole is even more dangerous than the sum of the parts."

Adam Tooze

In Tooze's work the phrase refers to international or global issues but the implications of a global polycrisis situation is beyond the scope of this conversation. Instead we will explore how the existence of this polycrisis situation affects us as individuals and leaders.

The interconnectedness of all things

While it is tempting for leaders to assume that political decisions, economic investments, natural disasters and wars in other parts of the world don't have any effect on their own circle of concern, it is becoming increasingly evident that the complexity of our connected world touches everyone. Here are some examples:

- Applying sanctions to Russia because of their actions in Ukraine affects agricultural exports and food prices.

- The eruption of the volcano Eyjafjallajökull in Iceland led to the grounding of air traffic across Europe for several days in 2010. The grounding of those flights had a domino effect on people across the world.

- The global financial crisis that started in the USA in 2008 had an effect on African countries' exports and falling commodity prices.

- The Fukushima Nuclear disaster in 2011 obviously affected Japan but also had an effect on global supply chains, the production of electronic components and impacted the automotive industry everywhere.

Leaders and organisations' response to poly crisis

Whereas in Toffler's work we see how people are stressed by an increasing rate of change in their lives, Poly Crisis implies stress that comes from uncertainty of the future, even the near future.

It takes an agile, open minded and flexible leader with good adaptive strategies to successfully lead an organisation in a complex, connected world in poly crisis.

The Pace - Complexity Graph

Illustration 1

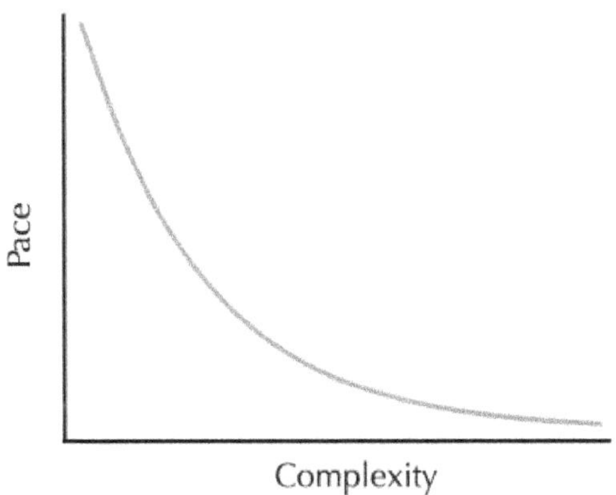

Future Shock causes stress because of the rapidly increasing pace of change. Poly Crisis causes stress because of the insane complexity of the world.

Our ability to live and work well is affected by how we respond to the combination of pace and complexity, to shock and crisis.

If our problems are complex we are going to have to slow down to address them. If we need to move fast, then we are not going to be able to address the nuances of complex issues.

Determining our place on this graph is a good way to visualise the competing stresses and to begin to navigate away from them.

Chapter 4: Coping Strategies for the Future

School Days

A few years ago my family moved and we had to place my daughter in a new school. A few months in we realised that she was not at all happy where she was and so we started talking with her and her teachers to find out what the problem was. When we sat with the school counsellor we saw the problem. The counsellor said that "to survive in this school a pupil needs to have a strong friend support base". Obviously as a new pupil she hadn't yet developed any significant friendships but our concern was with the very casual expectation from the counsellor that a child would need to 'survive'. School should be a place of learning, discovery, creativity, connection. It shouldn't be the first stage of toughening young people up so that they can cope with the rest of the fast paced rat race in their lives.

Unless, of course, that is our intention. If we want to prepare children for the extreme competitiveness of life then maybe the school should see that as their responsibility. But if we want to prepare children to more than cope, to eventually thrive in their lives, then lets not succumb to mere coping strategies.

Learning to Cope and Adapt

There are broadly two ways that we can respond to these changes into the future - we employ either adaptive or coping strategies.

Coping strategies are the immediate, short term and reactive responses to challenges. They happen after the event or stress inducing situation and are often executed without conscious thought. They include resistance to change, overwork, inappropriate behaviours, and the development of victim or blame mentalities.

Adaptive strategies however, are the considered and measured, longer term and proactive preparation for the future, or for a challenge.

The difference is clear when we consider the classic threat of a lion. Picture it: one person relies on an outdated 'run for it' strategy hoping that their sprint skills are worthy of the Olympics. They're not. He is going to be eaten, no matter how motivated he is! But his savvy friend who foresaw the potential for the arrival of a lion has a range of adaptive responses prepared: a fast getaway car, a concealed weapon, or perhaps they would have taken a scenic route to their destination to avoid the threat completely.

In the workplace, maladaptive coping strategies can harm employee mental and physical health. It can result in inefficiencies and lower productivity and engagement. Team leads resort to threatening behaviours, or dismissal of problems and the inability to recognise imminent crises. There is an avoidance of the real issues and a doubling down on busy work that has nothing to do with the imminent threats. Employees try to work ever faster instead of being provided with tools to work better.

Dimming Dreams - The example of Eskom's failure to act

To explore the real world consequences of bad coping strategies versus proactive adaptive strategies, let us have a look at some examples from the world of energy production.

The South Africa state owned power utility Eskom is a sad example of an organisation that failed to take proactive action, and whose coping strategies are painful demonstrations of too little action, too late and in the wrong direction. Ageing infrastructure that requires extensive repairs, the failure to build new power generation facilities, financial troubles and leadership challenges, corruption and governance issues created a situation where the country of South Africa simply does not have sufficient power to cope with demand. There are legal cases of people sabotaging the already failing infrastructure to win business contracts to repair their own actions and the former chief of Eskom, planning to make public corruption charges, was poisoned with cyanide in his coffee. The attempted murder case is just part of the billions of South African Rands worth of corruption, accusation and scandal that is at the heart of this enterprise's inability to function.

The coping strategy employed to manage this problem is a schedule of planned power outages, or load shedding, that leave different parts of the country without power for anything from 2 or 4 hours at a time. This schedule can ramp up to daily outages, sometimes to as many as 3 sessions in a day.

The impact is tremendous. Even with reduced supply of electricity, the tariffs for the consumers have increased. There is a huge economic impact for the country, for investment opportunities from wary multi-nationals who won't risk starting a new venture in South Africa, and for the companies, small business, retail and health service providers that have to find ways to operate without power on a regular basis. The only businesses doing well are those selling generators or power banks. The diminished public trust now extends to all state-owned enterprises and power generation has become an alarming political issue.

Eskom does have some forward looking projects including new power plants, development of smart grid technologies, renewable energy integration (this is a sun-drenched part of the world) and the reduction of carbon emissions, but for people in South Africa today, it is too little, too late. Their adaptive strategies, to be relevant and viable in the future, are eclipsed by the necessary coping strategies to just literally keep the lights on.

Energy and Environment Innovation

In comparison let's look at the energy programs in other parts of the world to see proactive and adapting responses.

Norway's Hydropower

Taking advantage of their abundant water resources, and centuries of experience, Norway has developed a sophisticated energy program that supplies the entire country with power and has some left over for export. Their future plans are to increase efficiency and sustainability of their system and to reduce the environmental impact and satisfy their country's climate goals. Not only do they have a stable energy supply but their hydropower industry adds positively to Norway's economy.

Netherland's Wind Energy

Again taking advantage of natural conditions in and around Netherlands, the government as well as private companies and research institutions, have invested in wind technologies both on land and at sea. While there are some environmental concerns about the impact of these technologies on the environment, they are still a clean and efficient energy source, and there is constant research into how to lower impacts and meet the European Union's renewable energy goals.

South Korea's Smart Grid

While challenging high implementation costs, regulatory hurdles and resistance from consumers and other utilities, South Korea has invested heavily in their smart grid technology.

The smart grid is an integrated electrical system that can respond to electricity generation, distribution and consumption needs. It makes power distribution much more efficient and reliable. Smart metres and sensors can provide real time feedback to consumers as well as managers of the grid and can provide insight into how to balance the grid during peak demand periods. South Korea is also integrating renewable energy production into the grid.

The Cost of Poor Coping Strategies

These examples compare the belated response of Eskom, trying only to get through the present day's energy requirements, with the forward thinking and adaptive strategies of countries investing and innovating with natural resources and available technology.

The cost of responding too late and being reactive is affecting the entire country's economic progress and costing that state-owned entity alone, billions of Rands.

# Coping Strategies

Let us unpack Coping Strategies, often employed in the midst of a crisis and in reaction to events rather than in preparation. Under stress, with few resources, people may respond to challenges with any of these reactions.

Denial and Avoidance

Simply ignoring the problem, denying its problematic nature or potential consequences, or keeping busy with less critical tasks to avoid the real issue, are time-honoured ways that we humans deal with issues we don't want to face.

Retreat to Tradition

This is a retreat, not to the carefully nurtured culture of an organisation, but to the 'We've always done it this way!' response.

Resistance to Change

Even in the face of evidence of how a change will be positive, stressed individuals will cling to old models and resist or undermine any attempt to evolve.

Catastrophizing

This cognitive distortion is when people dive deeply into the worst case scenario and cannot keep issues in proper proportion to their consequences. Instead of having a challenge that can be addressed, it becomes a calamity that spells ruin.

Cognitive Paralysis

While we believe that we want a number of choices of actions to cope with a problem, getting stuck in analysis paralysis prevents us from choosing and acting on the correct option, or indeed, any option.

Blame and Externalization

This is a common response to a problem, to immediately deflect responsibility to others and not to take ownership of an issue. Of course many big futures problems are not of our own making but by pointing fingers to others we also sacrifice the opportunity to find solutions or responses within ourselves.

Impulsivity

We know that we need to take action but a knee-jerk reaction, taken without significant thought or preparation can make a problem worse.

Physical and Mental symptoms

There are clear concerns for an organisation where the humans are operating in coping mode, but those individuals also suffer physical, emotional and mental symptoms of stress and anxiety that lower their chances of operating at peak performance levels and increase their chances of long term ill health.

Positive Coping Strategies

Not all coping strategies are negative. There are some positive actions people can take including meditative processes to calm themselves and problem solving steps to address the problem in a healthy way.

But it is far better to have developed Adaptive Strategies ahead of these issues. No matter how sophisticated an organisation is, or how many billions of dollars might run through their accounts, all organisations are run by humans, and when those humans are not prepared then they run the risk of acting irrationally and making seriously sub-par decisions.

Teaching Thriving

After understanding the primary motives of my daughter's original school, we moved her to a new one, in the middle of term. Her new classmates welcomed her and celebrated her birthday with her only two days after arriving there. The teachers were warm, yet challenging. The expectation was to build a person of character, someone who would go on to do beautiful things in the world. One week after joining this school my daughter was happy, singing show tunes and eager to get to school the next day.

We don't have to accept that coping is the best we can do. There is more beyond that.

The Pace - Complexity Graph

Illustration 2

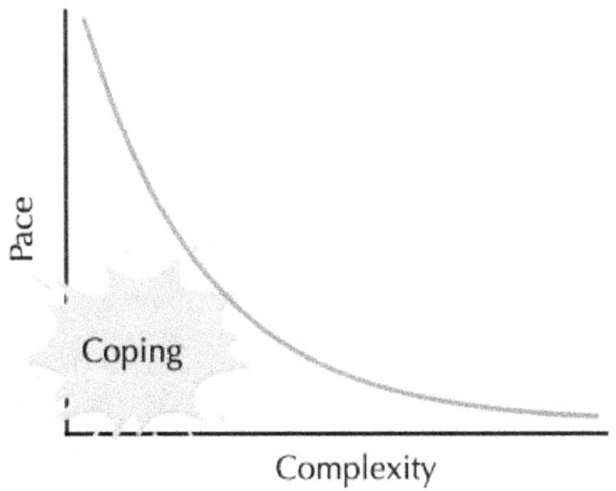

When facing any combination of pace and complexity in our lives, our first response is to find ways to cope. Anything below this curved line is a Coping Strategy. Not all Coping Strategies are inherently bad, but none will help us progress beyond the line. For that we need to step back and learn Adaptive Strategies.

Chapter 5: Developing Adaptive Strategies

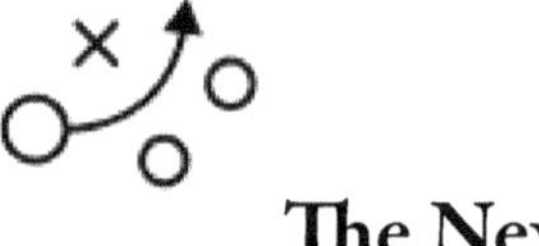

The Next Stage

To adapt is to respond to changing circumstances and find new ways of anticipating the future. Being rigid and inflexible in our thinking will lead to disaster. We need to be able to move and respond, to grow and to change.

These Adaptive Strategies are more proactive than coping strategies. Which means that we need to develop these competencies before we need them.

Adaptive Strategies - Individuals

In comparison to Coping Strategies, Adaptive Strategies provide positive and engaging ways to manage the changes that are imminent. These strategies are for both individuals and where appropriate, for organisations. Developing these strategies as a corporate culture can improve the chances of success for both humans and organisation.

Lifelong Learning

This should be a given. With the world developing exponentially fast, our education needs to be constantly updated. This does not have to mean academic education but certainly it means staying informed, attending courses, seminars and conferences and reading new publications on one's topic of interest, and beyond. This is a commitment to personal and professional development in order to remain relevant.

Anticipation and Scenarios

Anticipating the future is an effective way of preparing for changes. Just by considering how things may change opens our minds to new ideas and helps us prepare both personally as well as with practical plans and strategies to address a range of potential outcomes.

Flexibility and Resilience

Professionals who cultivate flexibility and resilience in their personal lives are better prepared to face changes, even unwanted ones, in the workplace. Without that flexibility, responses will be predictable, brittle and the opposite of innovative.

Networks and Communities

The world is much more connected than it has ever been before, which means that an organisation's reach is vaster and networks are broader. This can encourage collaboration in the face of the future and from those collaborations comes innovative thinking.

Diversification

It is easy for a modern professional to become expertly focussed on a narrow or niched field. While this is often given as career advice, to be the go-to expert on a subject, the professional who has little else in their resumé runs the risk of being made redundant if a significant update is made in their field either from artificial intelligence or some other application. We need to develop a breadth to our skills so that we can shift when necessary.

Challenge the algorithms

Our newsfeeds and Google searches are not the only areas of our lives affected by algorithms. The patterns of choice and behaviour that we naturally fall into affects every part of our lives including how we make decisions about money, time, ethics, social groups, our personal health and how we learn and go about problem solving. We couldn't get through the day without relying on some of those automated, unconscious decision making rules happening without intentional thought. But we do need to pause occasionally and be intentional about uncovering why we decide as we do, and then updating our personal algorithms as required. This happens when we learn new insights that allow us to make better decisions or when we evolve in our ethical or moral positions.

Adaptive Strategies - Organisations

Organisations and countries can also develop positive Adaptive Strategies.

Innovation and Adaption

A culture of innovation needs to be nurtured in an organisation. This necessitates a more collaborative, open and risk-taking approach to work, which is the opposite of cultures that are based on a fear of failure, resistance to change and rigid, hierarchical, siloed mentalities.

Diversification of the obvious as well as of strategy

Homogeneous organisations are poor in terms of the creativity that a diverse workforce would bring. But beyond seeking diversity in people, ideas and languages, a company should also consider a diversity of strategies or directions. This doesn't necessarily mean that a company has to pursue projects outside of their specialisation, but it does mean that they are ready to respond when necessary, just like Peugeot moved on from manufacturing coffee mills to manufacturing cars, and Samsung from dried fish and groceries to electronics and Nokia from a paper mill to cellphones and electronics.

Adaptive Policy Making and Governance

When every part of an organisation has been challenged by changes, leadership cannot hold on to redundant policies, outdated governance models and inappropriate values. There are some very innovative responses as examples:

• New Zealand focuses on a Wellbeing Budget to measure their progress rather than the old-fashioned GDP.

• Estonia pioneered an approach to E-Governance, simplifying and integrating citizens' experience of government by providing efficient digital services.

If people need to embrace the future, then so too do our organisations.

Sustainable Practices

Regardless of the push back by anti-woke activists, attention and investment in nurturing sustainable practices and good governance is both necessary and sort of ironically, profitable. While the effort of individuals is a small contribution, it takes action at national level for real change to happen. The country of Bhutan is regarded as the first carbon-negative country in the world and their government evaluates proposals and balances economic development against their commitment to sustainable activities. The country enjoys energy security and exports energy from their hydropower plants, they involve the community and society in the stewardship of their natural and cultural resources and they enjoy both a high Gross National Happiness index and a favourable tourism market.

Lurching or Leveraging

Without developing adaptive strategies we run the risk of lurching from crisis to crisis instead of leveraging the momentum of change to create something new and extraordinary.

"To survive, to avert what we have termed future shock, the individual must become infinitely more adaptable and capable than ever before. We must search out totally new ways to anchor ourselves, for all the old roots - religion, nation, community, family, or profession - are now shaking under the hurricane impact of the accelerative thrust."
Alvin Toffler

Chapter 6: Preparing for Uncertainty

The sad lament

The saddest lament I hear is 'There's nothing we can do'. It comes in various guises:

- We have no choice.
- What can one do?
- There's no alternative.
- There's no way around it
- It's always been done this way.
- It's too late to change now.

There is an effective way for us to recognise difficult life lessons and that is to see them in popular media. In 'Dead Poets Society', Robin Williams' character, the teacher John Keating, offers his students a new way to look at poetry, literature and ultimately life. Every time I watch the movie I experience the same heart ache of seeing young people glimpsing a chance to craft a meaningful life and then the overbearing responses of parents and teachers in opposition to that self expression. Beyond the tragedy of the main characters, the loss of life and destroyed careers, is the realisation that the parents and teachers who stifled the boys did so out of love. The only way they knew how to love their children and prepare them for the future, was to do what was traditionally done, only more so. They doubled down on rules and grades and conformity.

In the face of an unknowable future we often turn to the comfort of traditions. But traditions that worked in the past are irrelevant to the future.

While clearly there are some benefits to those who can rise to the top of a tight and traditional class structure, for most people they are simply enslaved. The rules will keep them in line but will never help them to succeed. And if they will not succeed while obeying the rules, why not risk a little imagination and fun along the way.

Tools for Crafting the Future

I am part of a family of very creative people. While I can't draw realistic stick figures I express my creativity in other ways. My mother and my daughter are very creative and have all the tools of their various hobbies, from painting, drawing, moulding, wood work, and more. If you step into their space you will find an amazing (and expensive) collection of tools. Whatever they set their hearts to creating today can be done because they have the tools and resources to start that project.

When I see people struggle with emotional paralysis and complain that there is nothing that they can do, I know that they just don't have the right tools. Maybe they aren't even aware of the tools that are available. As my family's artistic expression matures they obtain more sophisticated tools. These same tools are useless in my hands but in theirs, well they create magic.

I don't want anyone to feel like they have no options. Knowing that there are alternative ways to view a situation, a range of tools to change circumstances, role models of others who demonstrate what they have overcome, knowing this means that a person can develop hope that their situation can be changed. And hope fuels our willingness to do the difficult task of learning a new tool and crafting something significant.

What follows are ideas and tools and models that are available for us to proactively create adaptive strategies to overcome the shock and crisis, to move beyond coping and ultimately towards thriving.

Failure to respond

We all know the business school examples of major brands that failed to adapt and became synonymous with leadership lacking foresight. A McKinsey study demonstrated how the average lifespan of successful businesses listed on the S&P 500 used to be 61 years. It is now less than 18 years and by 2027 they estimate that 75% of these top valued companies will cease to exist.

The rate of change, introduction of new technologies, changes in delivery of value and changes in the demands of customers, in addition to world wide drivers of change, all play their part in the shortening life span of even top companies.

Various Models

It is not necessary to prepare for every eventuality. When we learn to use tools for leadership, management and business we give ourselves more capacity to think about the challenges. We learn that not only are there many tools and models available but that if one doesn't work, we can put it down and try another. When we have that freedom to experiment, our capacity to cope with challenges and to anticipate the future gets so much more creative and expansive.

I am tempted at this point to list every futures model and business tool that I can think of, almost to prove my argument that there must be something for everyone. But part of the journey of discovering what works, is to go on the journey yourself to find them.

But why not have a little taste of what's out there.

Adaptive Leadership Model

> Unlike routine problems, complex issues cannot be solved by a simple application of a set of rules. Adaptive Leadership develops the kind of leader who is willing to explore the real origins of an issue, are open to learning and understanding the implications of actions, and can afford a little experimentation in addressing the problem.

Resilience Frameworks

Developing resilience is more than an instruction to 'grin and bear it' or to get tough and show grit. Just as buildings need to be constructed to be resilient to the environment and climate, leaders can use resilience frameworks to mitigate risks, prevent unnecessary problems and be better at recovery after a crisis.

Crisis Management Models

A broad life-cycle of a crisis can look like this:

1. Before crisis preparation
2. Experience of crisis
3. Response and learning after crisis

There are many domain specific versions of crisis management models but the essential insights in terms of futures thinking is to intentionally anticipate potential problems, develop or design responses to those problems and then take relevant action when necessary and to learn, grow and repeat.

Antifragility

Coined by Nassim Taleb in his book "Antifragile: Things That Gain from Disorder", antifragility isn't just about withstanding knocks but it demonstrates how businesses can grow and thrive when designed to develop within chaos. Taleb advocates certain characteristics of an antifragile organisation:

- Resilience to stressors

- Developing robustness

- Non-linear decision making

- Decentralised systems

- Redundancies

- Evolutionary fitness

Change management models

Change management is an interesting place to observe the psychological responses to the future and the reluctance to change. From a fear of the unknown, to a sense of loss of control and perceived threats of loss, people can undermine their own opportunities in the future by resisting change in the present.

Change management is actually at the heart of our conversation about Future Shock and Poly Crisis: how we manage change is a measure of how we will fare in the future.

Change can come in many forms; as something huge, life altering, majorly disruptive; or as a slow, subtle shift to a different way of being. It can be self-initiated or imposed. It can apply to individuals or to societies.

Equipped

Now that we have some tools to use to develop Adaptive Strategies, we are better equipped to succeed in the future. But lets add one more really effective tool to our toolset - Scenario Planning.

Chapter 7: Scenario Planning - A Response to Poly Crisis

A set of scenarios

One of the most impactful tools in the futurist's toolset is that of scenario planning and when dealing with the uncertainty of a poly crisis world, scenarios may begin to put frameworks around what we are facing.

Scenario planning is the development of a set of different responses or outcomes that we face given certain variables. The development of these scenarios can represent a significant amount of research and preparation to provide insights into different facets of an organisation including cash flow, logistics, resource needs and supply chain impacts. But it can also be a short exercise of a few hours with a team who needs to sketch out some direction.

A 3 way Scenario Planning example

A simple way to begin with scenarios is to sketch out 3 perspectives: Best Case, Worst Case and the Middle of the Road option.

Middle of the Road

The Middle of the Road option is where we normally focus. This represents our business plans, regular forecasts or our natural expectations and relies on fairly predictable results with all the variables. Depending on the complexity of the exercise this could include cash flow expectations, human resource and talent requirements, availability of other resources, normal sales or income. A Middle of the Road scenario is sort of like last year, but better by 10%.

Best Case Scenario

When you anticipate the best possible results you are developing the Best Case Scenario. Sales go up. Input costs drop. You can afford to hire the best talent from anywhere in the world. Your product is a social media trending topic, for all the right reasons. Profits are through the roof!

Hopefully, even as you read that last paragraph your body and brain reacted as we expect them to react to good news. Our brains take the input of the thought of success as if it were real. Our brains cannot tell the difference between real and imagined so whatever we feed it, it believes. In the presence of this exciting, wonderful, successful news, our brain goes to work producing certain chemicals, in this case some heady combination of endorphins, dopamine and serotonin. That chemical cascade floods the body and the body reacts as expected: muscles relax, we smile, we feel energised, our pupils dilate and our breathing and heart rate slow down nicely.

In preparing a practical scenario focussed on everything going tremendously well, our brains and bodies act as if that has actually happened.

We want to let ourselves experience that brain-body-emotion situation and allow it to pass. Once it is over, we can turn our attention, not to imagining how we will spend all our profit and bonuses, but what we would need to do practically to prepare for this opportunity. Would we need an initial cash injection to pay for resources? Would we need new staff with specific skills or do we need to upskill existing staff? Would we need new skills ourselves? Would we need bigger premises, more equipment, warehousing, new outlets?

These questions do not necessarily need to be answered in detail. Depending again on the nature of the project, it could just be sketching out questions that should be asked, or conversations that could be had with team members. Simply being aware of the list of decisions that would need to be made should you experience such a windfall, is enough to satisfy the purpose of anticipating the future and preparing your thinking.

Worst Case Scenario

As expected, the Worst Case Scenario is the opposite of the Best. In this case we want to explore some of the situations that could cause huge problems for us. What if something happens next year that makes Covid look like child's play? What if AI makes most of the work we do redundant and we lose clients almost instantly, or staff become superfluous over night? What if new legislation, politics, or an environmental disaster makes our main products or services impossible to deliver?

Now just like in the Best Case Scenario, as you read this paragraph your brain and body react immediately. Your brain thinks that what you are thinking about is an imminent threat. Cortisol, adrenaline and norepinephrine are released in your brain to help your body cope with the fight or flight response. Our bodies are primed for action - heart rate goes up along with blood pressure. We become more alert, our muscles tense up and the skin starts to sweat to manage the crisis. Unnecessary functions slow down including digestion, reproduction and immunity.

Too many people live constantly in this 'worst case scenario' frame of mind. They experience too much stress, too frequently. This is meant to be a short term response to an imminent threat, not a lifestyle response to living in the world today.

That is why this exercise is actually so powerful. Much of the stress we experience is an unnamed, amorphous, vague threat. The very nature of not being able to name what makes us anxious increases our anxiety. But by settling down to face it, name it and contemplate the consequences actually reduces its horrible effect on our lives.

The ancient Stoics called this practice *Premeditatio Malorum* - a Premeditation of Evils. They would contemplate the end of their lives, their death, and consider what they might regret at their passing, what has been left undone. And after the exercise they would get up and go and live a better life for it.

Fire drill

If developing scenarios seems like a daunting prospect, consider how a well constructed escape route and fire drills help to keep us safe in the case of a disaster. Scenarios are our private fire drills, and even if we never have to use them, knowing and practising them develops a prepared mindset for any eventuality.

The Pace - Complexity Graph

Illustration 3

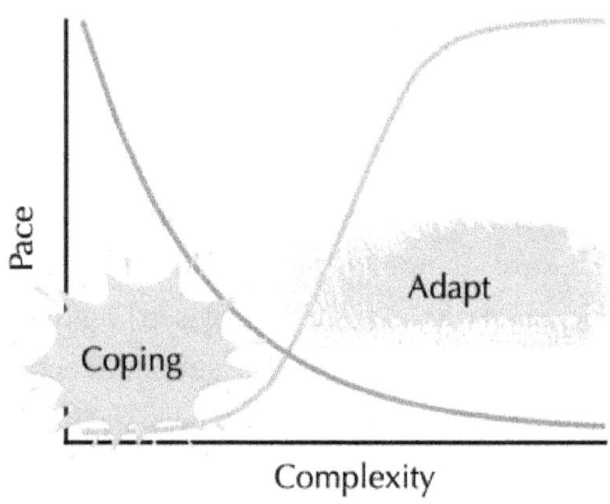

By intentionally adopting Adaptive Strategies we move above the line. We get ahead of our known and unknown challenges. We can begin to take advantage of opportunities offered to us because of disruptions instead of frantically trying to respond.

Chapter 8: Thrive

"If you do not change direction, you may end up where you are heading."
  Lao Tzu

 **Redefine. Craft. Thrive.**

As we learn to move beyond Coping Strategies and become familiar with Adaptive Strategies, we then begin to wonder what comes next. We can Thrive. We need to go through a process of Redefining some of our fundamental concept, then intentionally Craft new approaches and then enjoy the space where we Thrive.

Redefine

In almost every science fiction story that plays with the concept of time travel, there will be a conversation about the danger of going back in time, accidently doing something (which either involves a butterfly or a grandfather) that radically changes the course of history and which could very well mean that the person exploring the time continuum would never have been born.

We are not exploring the timey-wimey concept of time travel here. What we are doing is considering how our actions right now will affect the future. They will affect the future, whether we are proactive in creating something or complacent in accepting what is already happening around us.

A good futures thinking exercise is to think of a date in the future, and then imagine looking back on this current period you are in. Will that person viewing this time in history wish that you had done something different, something more, something intentional to avoid what they are experiencing at that point in the future? Or might they look back and celebrate these moments when we grasped the threads of time and wove a more preferable future.

Let us explore a few ways to intentionally Redefine our future.

Prophylactic Philosophy

Humans are the only species capable of philosophical reflection; of choosing world views, values and intentions. And yet in the busyness of life we so seldom take the time to do so. It's only when something interrupts our constant action that we stop to reflect. That interruption could be a retrenchment, an illness, a loss, a birthday ending in '0'. It could be that crisis on the brink of destroying our lives that demonstrates how fragile we are and ill equipped to face the future.

Prophylactic philosophy is an invitation to face that crisis before it is real, before it has the power to undermine us.

The Worst Case Scenario concept explored earlier provides one way to intentionally engage in reflection about what we might face in the future, and then gives us the time and space to take action to mitigate that scenario.

We can be Conscious Futurists

Just like we are all philosophical at our core, we are also all natural futurists. We all look to the future and wonder and hope and dream. But if we don't approach the future with some intention, then those hopes and dreams fade away. For some people hope will be replaced with anxiety and fear.

Recognising that we are natural futurists allows us to become intentional, Conscious Futurists. When we give ourselves that title we begin to take ownership of our choices and explore how we can create a better, more preferable future.

Change definition of success

If we do not intentionally define what success means to us, we unconsciously inherit a perspective from our society. We then frantically spend our lives measuring ourselves against this standard without ever having consciously defined what we actually wanted to do with our lives.

Africa's concept of 'ubuntu' and the Nordic cultures' expression of work/life balance contrast with the popular western capitalist version of success. Even Japan is working to overcome *karoshi,* the fetish of overwork and instead look to *ikigai,* the sweet spot at the intersection of what one loves, one is good at, what the world needs and what one can be paid for.

There are many ways to define personal or national success that we have perhaps not yet explored.

Challenge concepts of scarcity

The concept of scarcity is a useful tool for those who have influence over resources. In sales and politics it is used to put us in a defensive position. We need to protect what we have and struggle and strive to acquire more. In reality there is more than enough, of almost everything, for everyone. But that makes a poor economic model for modern society.

While we cannot necessarily address these big economic models, we can challenge the concept of scarcity in our lives and organisations. Many models show us how to do that including mindful consumption, conscious capitalism, circular economies, efficiencies and conservation, harmony with the environment and cooperation within communities.

An abundance mindset is the prerequisite for intentionally creating a future of thriving.

Identity

One of the worst mistakes we have made as western society is to enforce the concept of a binary identity. This is expressed in everything from politics (right / left), education (pass / fail), legislation (guilty / not guilty), language (good / bad), religion (believer / non-believer), economic class (rich / poor), international relations (nationalist / globalist) and of course gender and sexuality.

By forcing a choice to the extreme of these options we reinforce the concept of 'if you are not for me, you are against me'. That type of thinking is restrictive and disempowering.

There is a world of wonder to be found in the middle of these extremes. Expressions of creativity, co-creation, diversity, respect and honour dwell in the space where we allow ourselves and others to just be, as opposed to be defined.

Craft

Now that we have challenged previously unexplored assumptions of our current lives and what the future could be like, we need to start to craft that future. We begin to move past Adaptive Strategies and become more strategic and pioneering.

Develop futures thinking

A Futures Thinking mindset is the start of an intentional approach to the future. Instead of being trapped by our limited knowledge we are invited to explore the unknown. We need to continually learn and develop new skills. We can learn futures literacy, equipping ourselves with new language and concepts that give us more power to understand the uncertainty around us and to take purposeful action.

Futures Thinking is not an additional skill set that we apply on top of other skills in the workplace. Futures Thinking is a foundational approach to all of thinking. It is the salt that needs to be a part of the preparation of a meal, not simply sprinkled on top of a bland dish.

Find ways to incorporate a futures focussed mindset in every decision you need to make, and as you learn the tools and skills your mindset will shift to automatically thinking through this lens.

Foster a culture of authenticity

It is easy to dismiss authenticity as another buzz word in a world of constant marketing hype. However the courage to present ourselves as our authentic selves is a radical notion. To begin to craft an intentional future we need to understand who we are and what we want. Too often we accept the values of a consumer society or inherited values from our families without ever really considering them.

If we take the time to uncover our values, what is important to us, and then start to live according to those values we begin a profoundly beautiful journey towards the life we want to live.

Promote Conscious Leadership and Futures

Being 'conscious' means to be aware of, to pay attention to, to have values and ethics around something, to show empathy and to be able to adapt. With a working definition like this we should apply conscious thinking to every part of our lives. We can explore conscious leadership, conscious capitalism, conscious consumption, conscious education.

And of course we can become Conscious Futurists as well. We can be intentional about crafting a future that is inclusive and healing rather than one that is divisive and exclusionary.

Collaboration, Co-creation, Context

There are no self-made men. There are no lone heroes. We cannot craft a future alone and collaboration and co-creation become essential values to the crafting of any sustainable and valuable scenario.

While collaboration is about working together in a mutually beneficial way, co-creation goes further. When we co-create we put aside our own egos and ambitions to literally develop a plan with others. We explore what is possible. We bring our creativity and genius together with others to make something that is more than the sum of its parts, more than we could ever achieve on our own.

And that futures plan must be in context. We cannot import scenarios or models from one part of the world and apply them in a different context.

Encourage risk taking and curiosity

It may seem counterintuitive to advocate for risk taking in creating scenarios but safe, tried-and-tested approaches are guaranteed to fail with novel challenges. To be adaptive and agile means to explore approaches with the understanding that you will not get it right every time. There are no guarantees when we need to make up a new approach to a problem that has never been seen before. By developing curiosity in our thinking we increase our chance of creating a plan that will succeed.

"The most difficult thing is the decision to act, the rest is merely tenacity."
Amelia Earhart

Thrive

It is not enough for us to survive shock and crisis. It is not enough for us to merely keep ahead of the Coping line. We are designed to want more and to express meaning in our lives. We long for the opportunity to create something, to express something of ourselves.

And that is essentially what Thriving is all about: the chance to live in a world where we experience relative harmony, can work in collaboration with others to co-create beautiful, meaningful work.

This opportunity is not available to everyone, not in the world we live in today, so we who can should use this chance to design a more preferred future. In our scenarios we can develop various versions of the future and amongst those versions will be the one that honours people and planet, one that is collaborative, one that is designed to embrace more people. I hope that is the thriving future we are aiming towards.

"If we do not learn from history, we shall be compelled to relive it. True. But if we do not change the future, we shall be compelled to endure it. And that could be worse."
Alvin Toffler

The Pace - Complexity Graph

Illustration 4

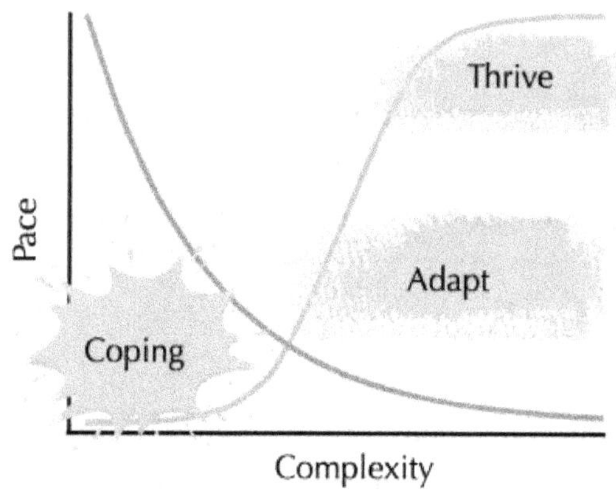

We begin to Thrive when we intentionally redefine our desires, develop our skill and craft a futures plan. We have moved away from the Pace / Complexity line and now operate in a unique space we have designed for ourselves.

Chapter 9: Charting Your Path in an Ever-Changing World

While we live in a world characterised by future shock and poly crisis, we can learn to intentionally develop more than coping strategies. We can develop adaptive strategies. We can move beyond the stress and crisis by adopting a futures focussed mindset and then we get to thrive.

The journey to change from coping to thriving is never going to be easy and neat, but it will be worth it. You get to chart your own path to the future and you no longer need to live to satisfy someone else's ambitions.

Not every person in the world today is experiencing Future Shock. Not every society is concerned with the global implications of the Poly Crisis.

And not everyone nor every organisation wants to reskill, refocus or realign themselves to remain relevant.

Business leaders are often seeking ways to help employees cope, be more productive, embrace the right changes and technologies or strategies so that they can keep up and reskill themselves so that they can remain relevant. But that presupposes that we all actually buy into this notion of constant growth to prop up a faulty capitalist society.

There are alternatives, perhaps radical ones, for individuals, businesses and countries willing to redefine how they rate themselves and pursue success.

As an informed futurist, you can now work on developing two strategies, two scenario schemes:

- How do you use adaptive strategies to keep up with change in your field so that you remain relevant, and simultaneously,

- How can you explore completely different ways of being human, experiencing this reality and expressing your natural creative talent.

While the opportunity to thrive and to express ourselves should be the right of every person, we know enough to understand that we who can are privileged and that there are many who are not in a position to do anything more than cope, or even just survive. It is my passionate belief that the more of us who do good futures work, the safer we make the future for more people. And safer, better, congruent, harmonious futures benefit more than just the inner circle. It means a better future for everyone.

"To be free is not merely to cast off one's chains, but to live in a way that respects and enhances the freedom of others."
Nelson Mandela

What Comes Next

You are now on an expedition to the future. Start thinking with a futures focussed mindset and developing your capacity for growth and learning. There are many tools and resources available online, and if you subscribe to the FuturesAlchemist.com website you will receive notifications about open webinars, online workshops, books and more.

You can find more books in this series of "Introduction to Futures Thinking".
- Chief Futures Thinking Officer
- Be the Conscious Futurist The World Needs Now
- Futures Literacy - The Professional Development Skill We Are Missing

Also by Charlotte Kemp:
Futures Alchemist - A Journey of Discovery to Co-Create Preferred Futures

This topic, as well as many others, is available as a keynote, webinar or in-person workshop. Please contact the author to explore how to tailor this content to meet your specific needs.

charlotte@futuresalchemist.com

"The future is already here. It's just not evenly distributed."
William Gibson

About the Author

Charlotte Kemp is a futurist keynote speaker, author and strategic foresight coach who works with organisations to co-create preferred futures. She is a Past President of both the Professional Speakers Association of Southern Africa (PSASA) and of the Global Speakers Federation (GSF) and maintains membership of the Association of Professional Futurists (APF).

Charlotte is also Chief Relationship Officer for Voices Into Africa, an events company seeking to raise the profile of speakers, events and collaborations across Africa.

Don't miss out!

Visit the website below and you can sign up to receive emails whenever Charlotte Kemp publishes a new book. There's no charge and no obligation.

https://books2read.com/r/B-A-GJAAB-ULRWE

BOOKS 2 READ

Connecting independent readers to independent writers.

Also by Charlotte Kemp

Futures Tools Series
Foresight Dictionary

Introduction to Futures Thinking
Futures Literacy. The Professional Development Skill We Are Missing
Become the Conscious Futurist the World Needs Now
From Future Shock to PolyCrisis

Watch for more at https://www.futuresalchemist.com/.

About the Author

Charlotte Kemp is the *Futures Alchemist*, a futurist keynote speaker who works with organisations to co-create preferred futures. She is a Past President of the Professional Speakers Association of Southern Africa (PSASA), maintains membership of the Association of Professional Futurists (APF) and serves as President of the Global Speakers Federation (GSF) 2023/24.

Charlotte is the author of a number of books, including 'Futures Alchemist' which presents a narrative of how to use her Map, Compass and Guide model to navigate unknown futures.

She is also the Chief Relationship Officer for Voices Into Africa, an events company seeking to raise the profile of speakers, events and collaborations across Africa.

Charlotte's signature talk is "Become the Conscious Futurist the World Needs, Now" and explores ways to intentionally create changes that will usher in our preferred future for our own industries.

Based in Cape Town, South Africa, Charlotte and her husband also love to travel and explore other parts of the world.

Read more at https://www.futuresalchemist.com/.

www.ingramcontent.com/pod-product-compliance
Lightning Source LLC
Chambersburg PA
CBHW050609160726
48003CB00003B/1110